The Best Of JAMES TAYLOR For Guitar

Includes SUPER-TAB Notation

D1571865

C O N T E N T S

Mockingbird

Words and Music by
INEZ and CHARLIE FOXX
Additional Lyrics by
JAMES TAYLOR

Moderately Rock

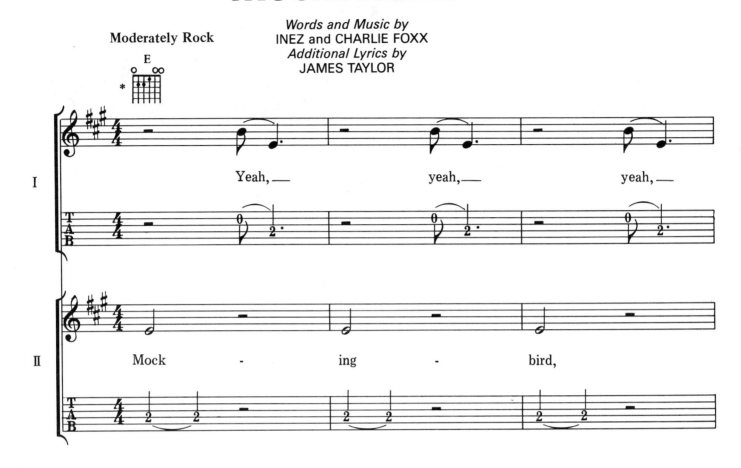

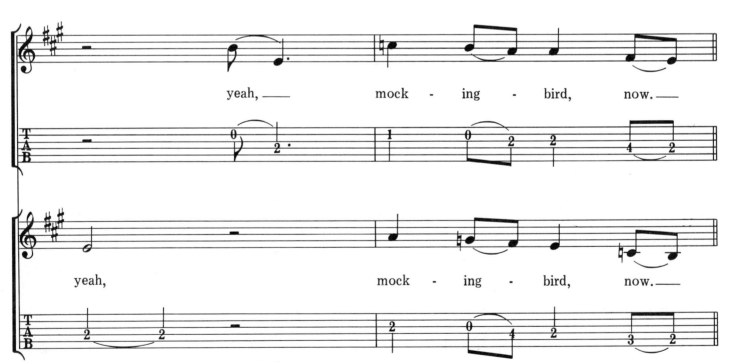

*To play along with recording, place capo at 6th fret.

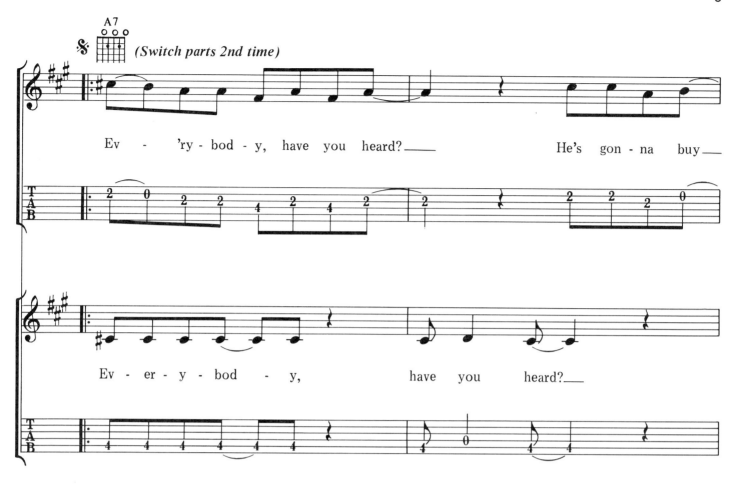

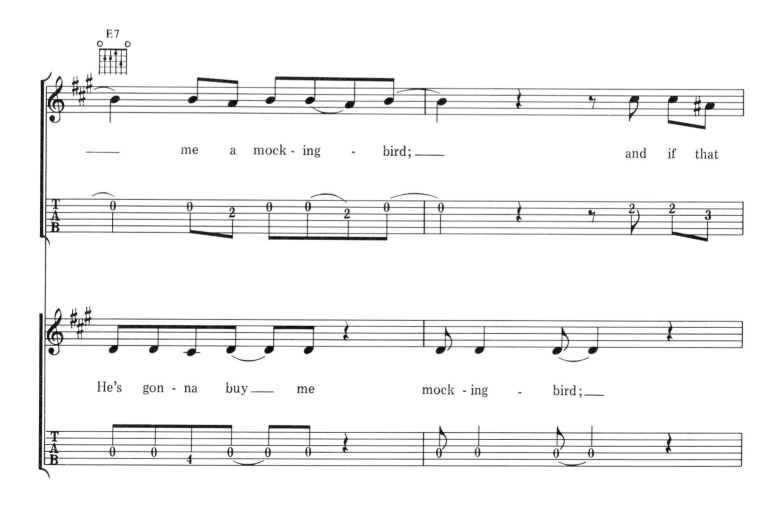

4

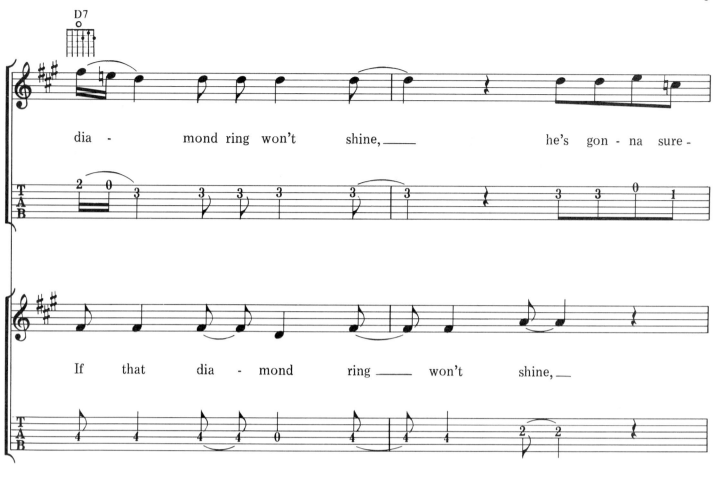

dia - mond ring won't shine,_____ he's gon - na sure -

If that dia - mond ring ___ won't shine, ___

ly break this heart of ___ mine._____ And that's

sure it's gon - na break this heart of mine._____ And that's

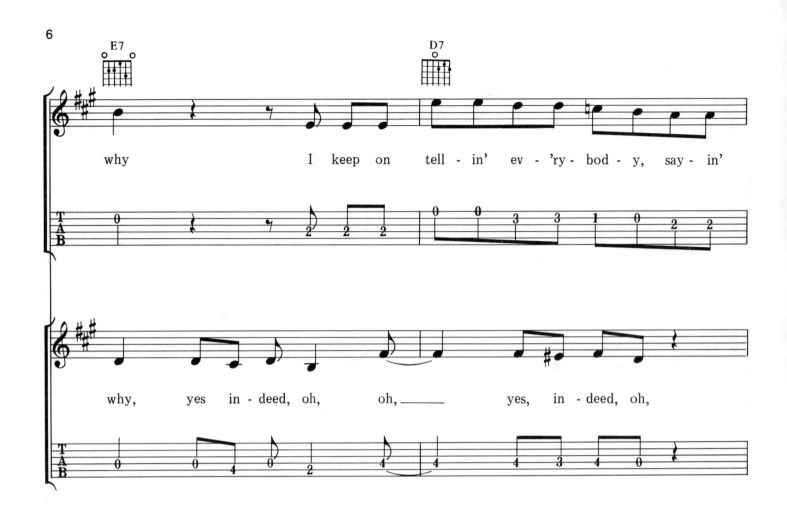

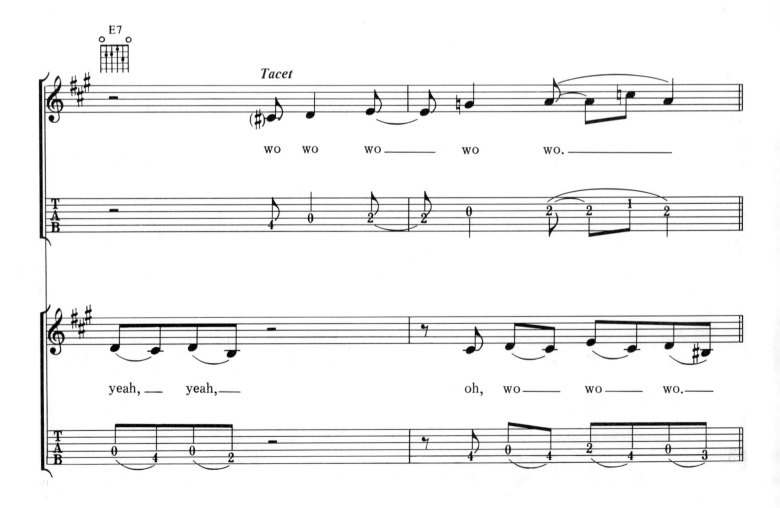

Hear me now and un - der - stand, _____ he's gon - na find ___

Hear me now _____ and un - der - stand, ___

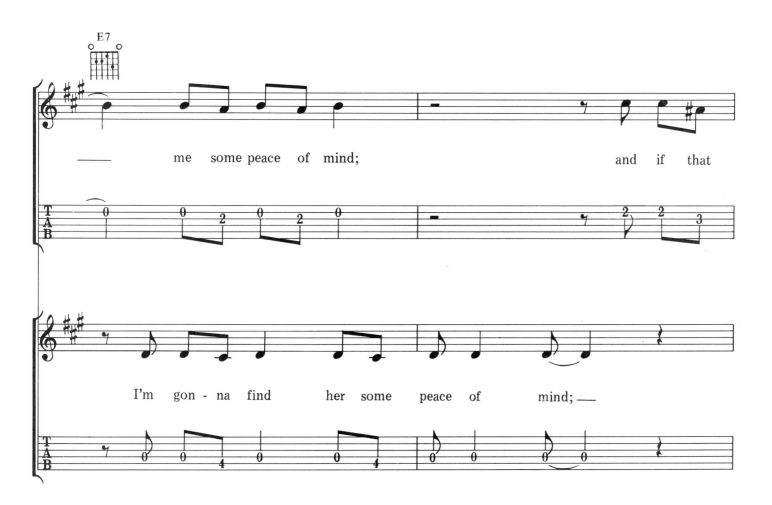

____ me some peace of mind; and if that

I'm gon - na find her some peace of mind; ___

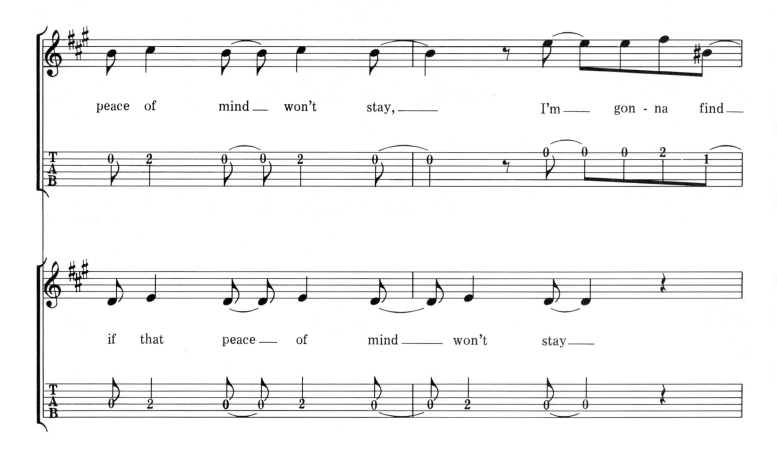

peace of mind___ won't stay,_____ I'm___ gon - na find___

if that peace___ of mind_____ won't stay___

___ my - self a bet - ter way.

And if that
I might

I'm gon - na find my - self a bet - ter_____ way._____

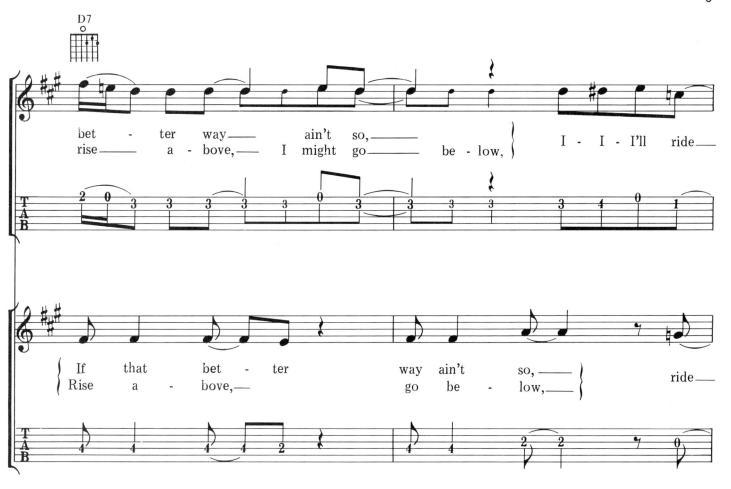

shout-in' in your ear,___ say-in'   wo wo wo___ wo wo.___

___   yes in-deed, oh,   yeah,___yeah,___   oh, wo___ wo___ wo.___

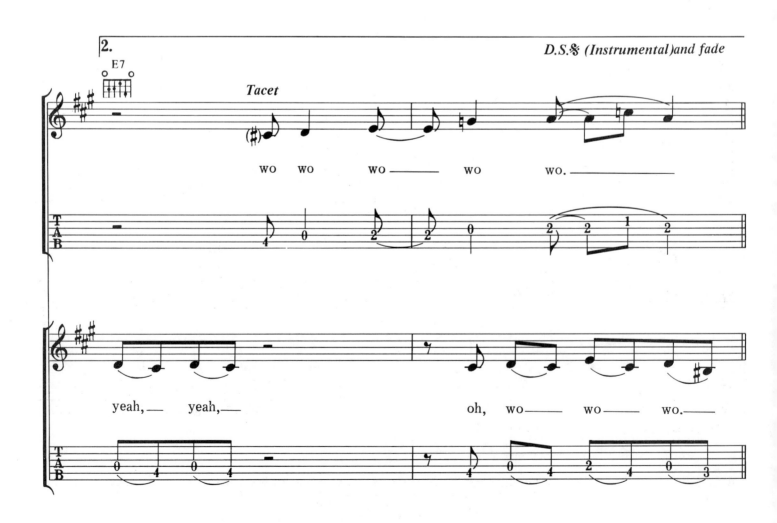

wo wo wo ___ wo wo. ___

yeah,___ yeah,___   oh, wo___ wo___ wo. ___

Fire And Rain

Words and Music by
JAMES TAYLOR

*To play along with recording, place capo at 3rd fret.

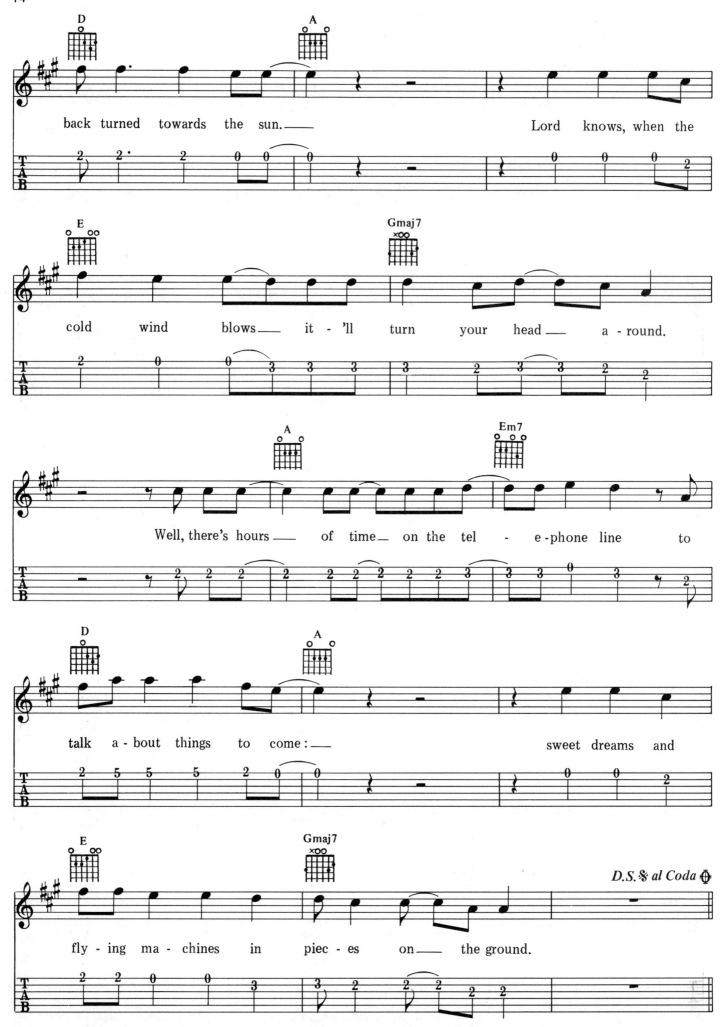

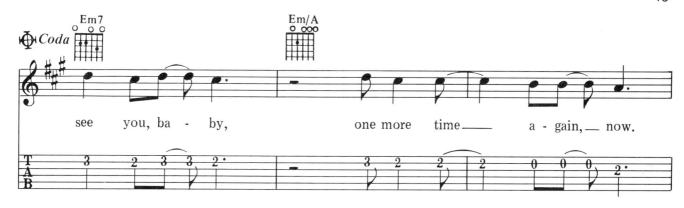

see you, ba - by, one more time —— a - gain, —— now.

Thought I'd see —— you one more time —

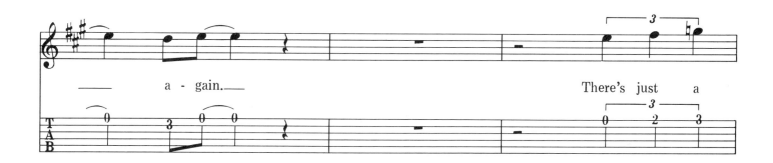

—— a - gain. —— There's just a

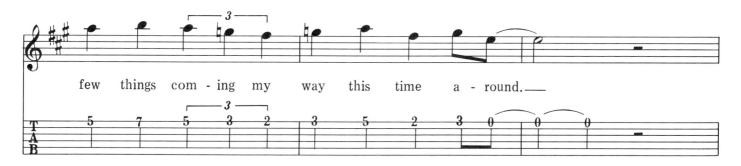

few things com - ing my way this time a - round. ——

Repeat and fade (vocal ad lib.)

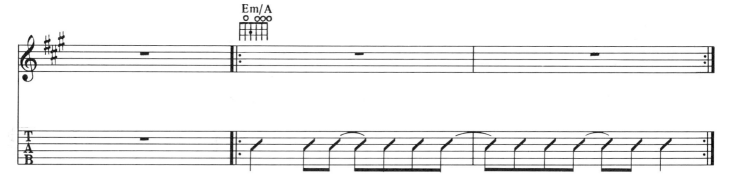

Shower The People

Words and Music by
JAMES TAYLOR

*To play along with recording, place capo at 3rd fret.

Repeat and fade(with lead vocal ad lib.)
N.C. (Guitar repeats previous 4 bars)

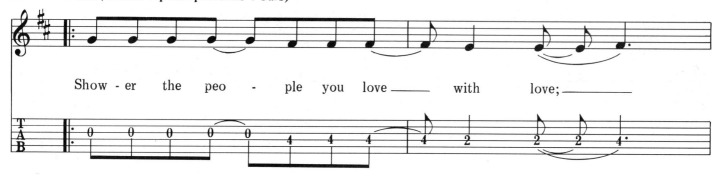

Show - er the peo - ple you love ———— with love; ————

show them the way ——— that you feel. ——————————

Vocal Ad Lib

They say in every life,
They say the rain must fall.
Just like a pouring rain,
Make it rain.
Love is sunshine.

Sweet Baby James

Words and Music by
JAMES TAYLOR

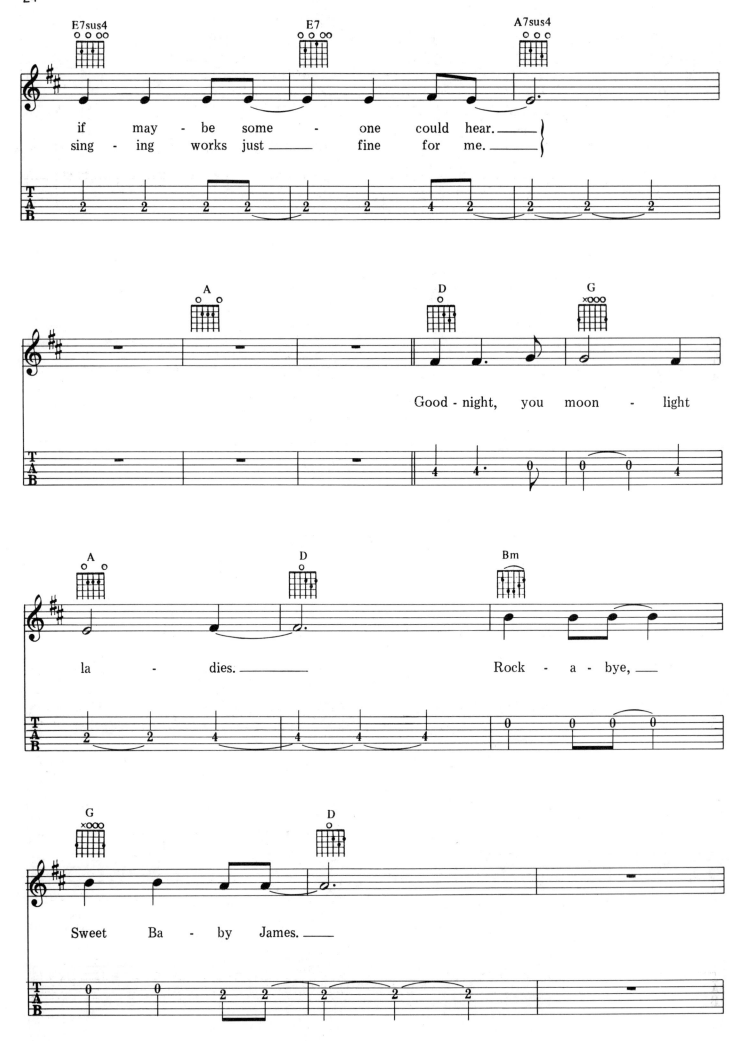

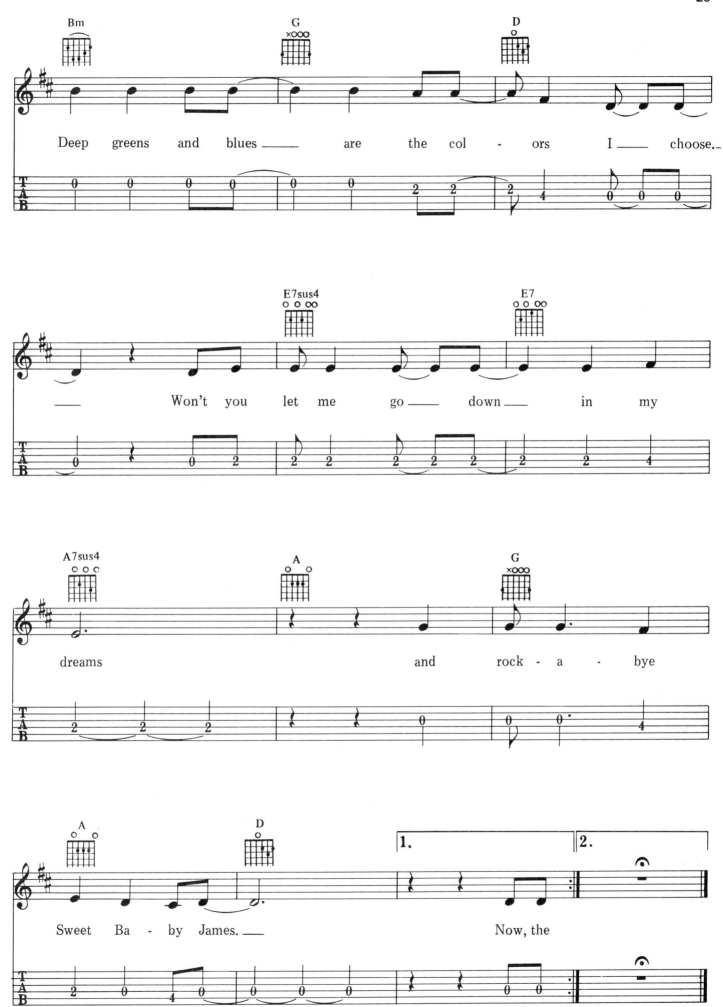

You've Got A Friend

Words and Music by
CAROLE KING

(Instrumental)

When you're down —

and trou - bled and you
a - bove ____ you should turn

need a help - ing hand, ____ and
dark and full of clouds, ____ and that

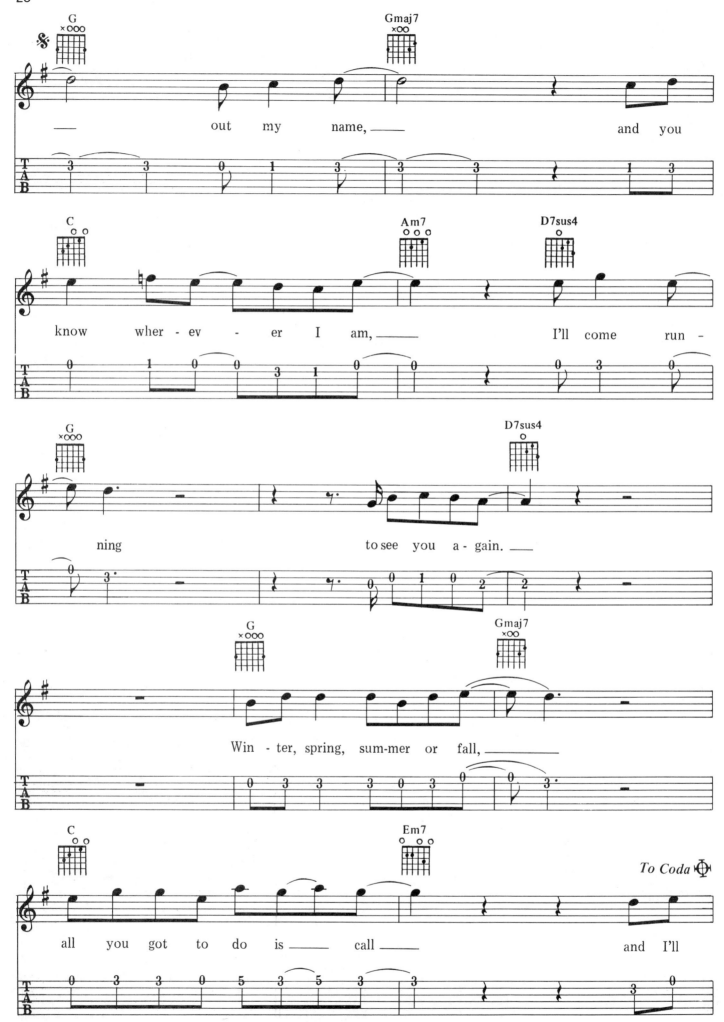

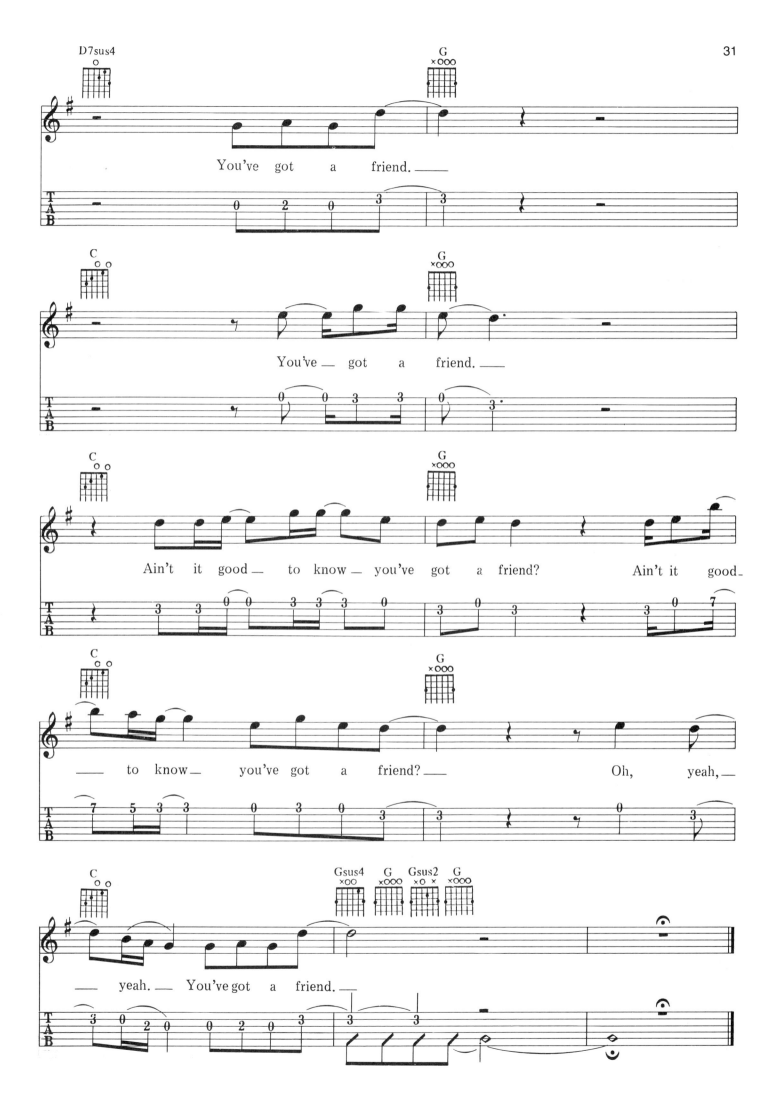

Don't Let Me Be Lonely Tonight

Words and Music by
JAMES TAYLOR

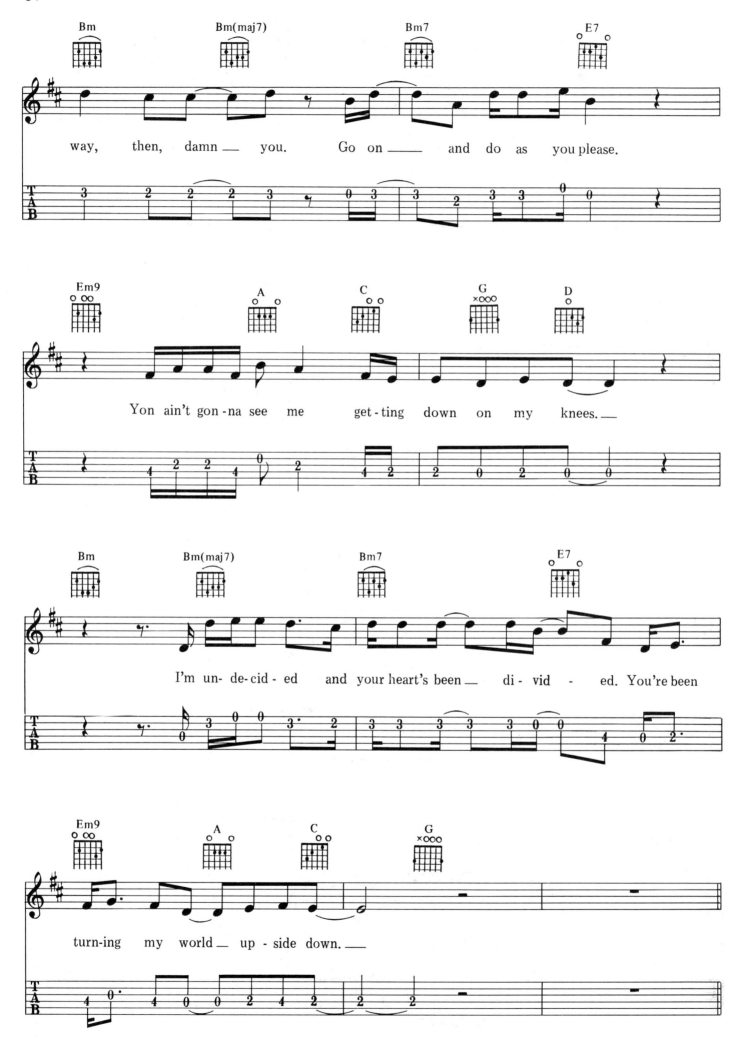

Her Town Too

Words and Music by
JAMES TAYLOR, JOHN DAVID SOUTHER
and WADDY WACHTEL

1. She's been a-fraid ____ to go out. ____
2. 3. *See additional lyrics*

she's a-fraid ____ of the knock ____ on her door. ____

____ There's al-ways a shade ____ of a doubt. ____

She can nev-er be sure ____

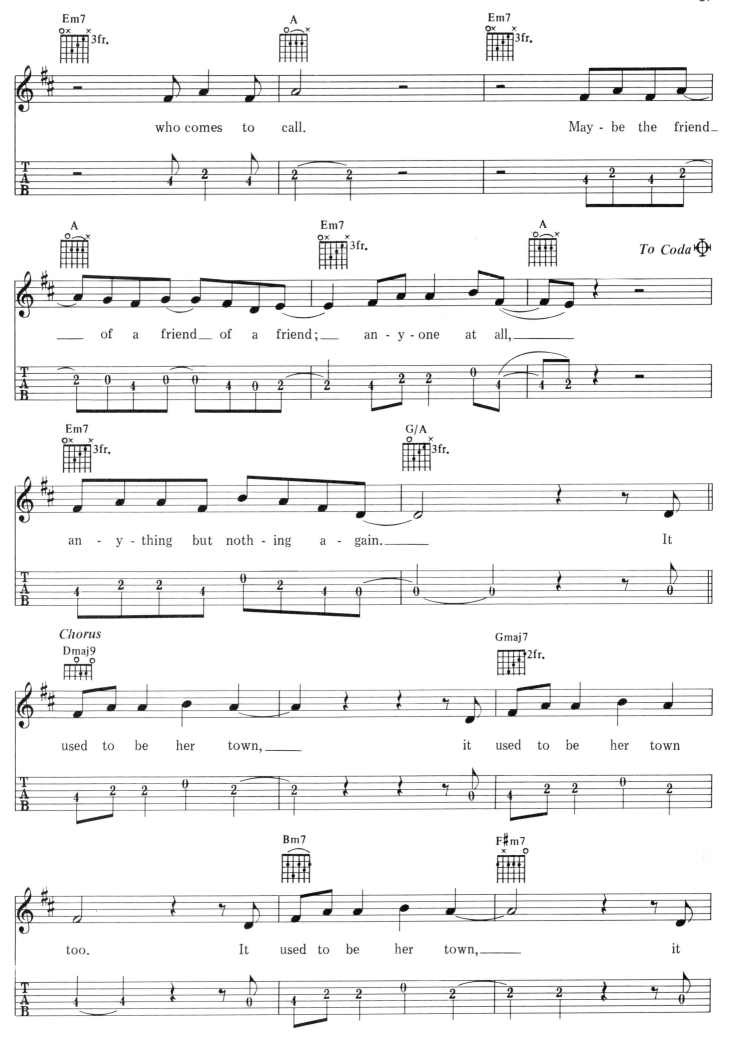

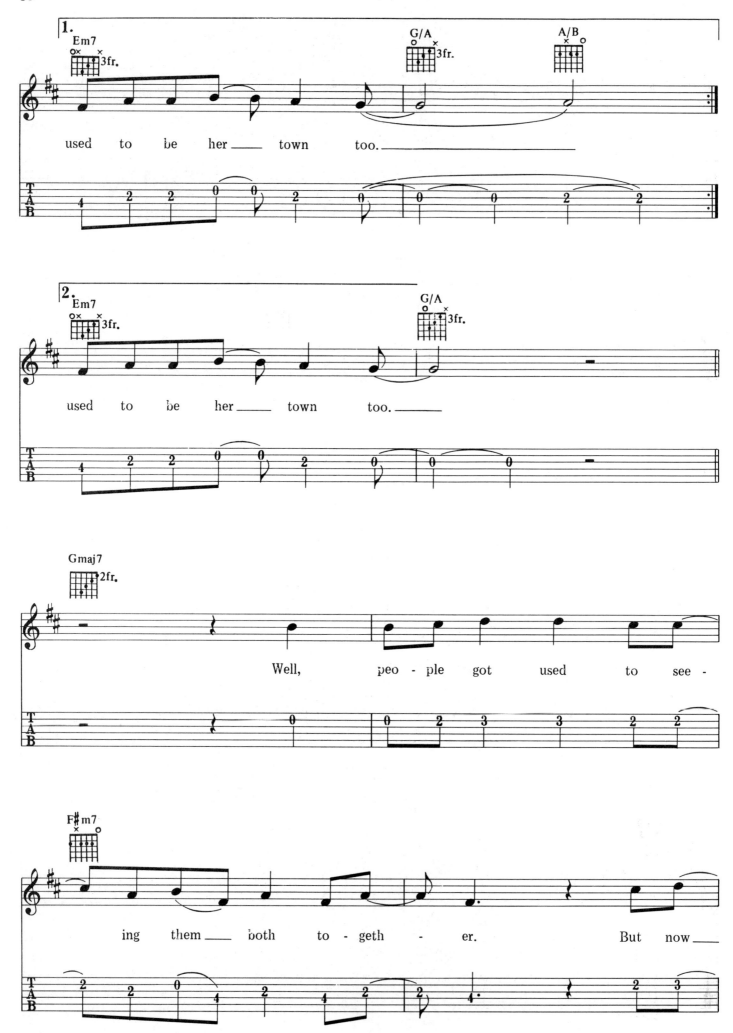

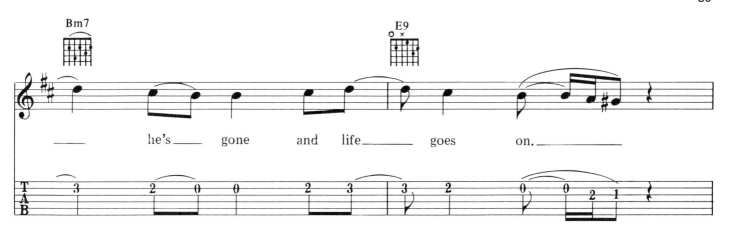

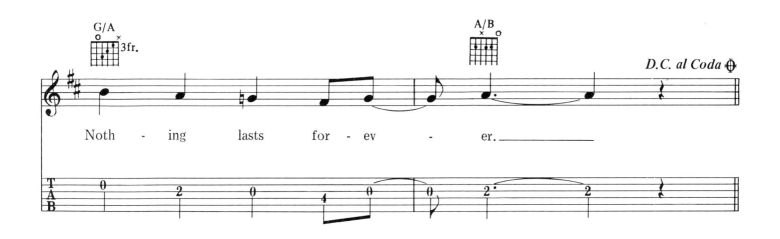

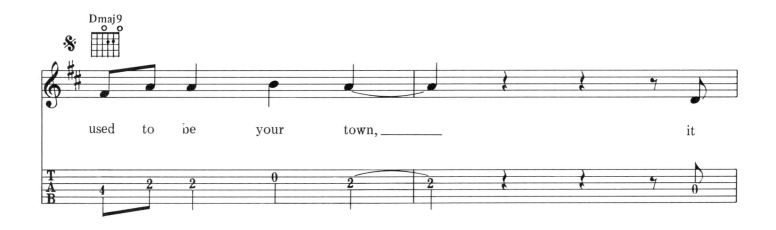

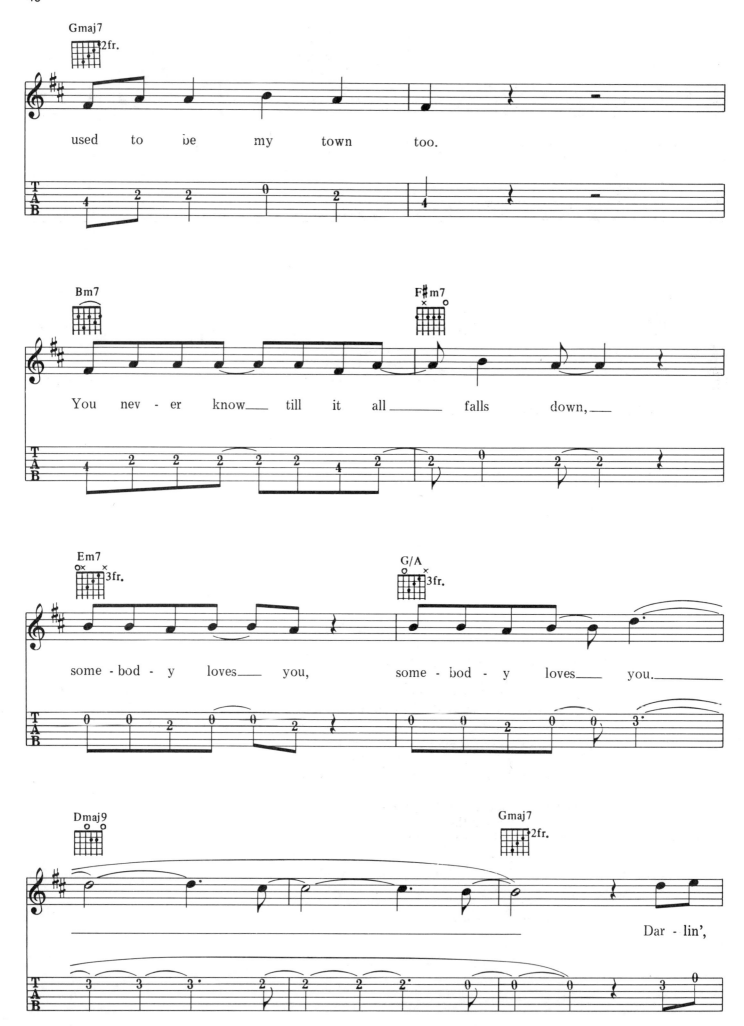

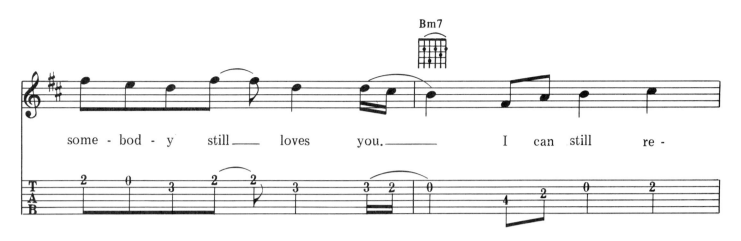

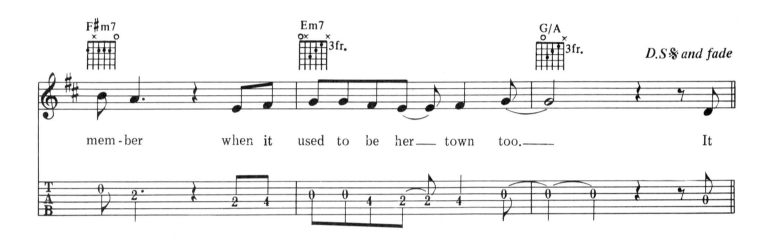

D.S.%and fade

Additional Lyrics

2. Seems like even her old girlfriends
   Might be talking her down.
   She's got her name on the grapevine,
   Runnin' up and down the telephone line,
   Talkin' 'bout someone said, someone said somethin' 'bout somethin' else
   Someone might have said about her.
   She always figured that they were her friends,
   But maybe they can live without her. *(To Chorus)*

3. She gets the house and the garden.
   He gets the boys in the band,
   Some of them his friends, some of them her friends.
   Some of them understand.
   Lord knows that this is just a small-town city.
   Yes, and everyone can see you fall.
   It's got nothing to do with pity.
   I just wanted to give you a call.

That's Why I'm Here

Words and Music by
JAMES TAYLOR

*To play along with recording, place capo at 3rd fret.

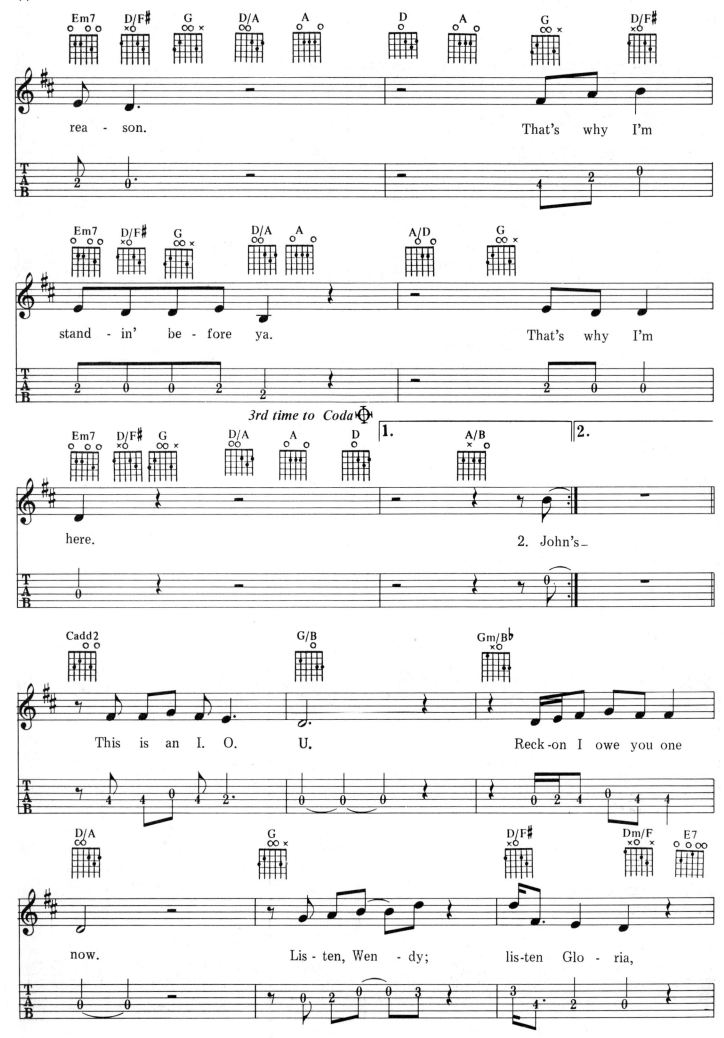

3rd time to Coda

ADDITIONAL LYRICS

2. John's gone, found dead. He dies high; he's brown bread.
   Later said to have drowned in his bed.
   After the **laughter**, the wave of dread.
   It hits us like a **ton** of lead.
   It seems they're not to burn, means they turn on a dime.
   And walk on if you're walking even if it's an uphill climb.
   Try to remember that working's no crime.
   Just don't let 'em take your wasted time.

   That's why I'm here.
   There'll be no more message tonight.
   That's why I'm here.
   That's why I'm here.

3. Oh, fortune and fame, such a curious game.
   Perfect strangers can call you by name
   And pay good money to hear "Fire and Rain"
   Again and again and again.
   Oh, some are like summer, comin' back every year.
   Got your baby, got your blanket, got your bucket of beer.
   I break into a grin from ear to ear
   And suddenly it's perfectly clear.

   That's why I'm here.
   Singin' tonight, tomorrow and every day.
   That's why I'm **standin'**
   That's why I'm here.

Handy Man

Moderately slow

Words and Music by
OTIS BLACKWELL
and JIMMY JONES

Hey girls, gath - er 'round.

Lis - ten to what I'm put - tin' down.

Hey ba - by, I'm your han - dy man.

I'm not the kind to use a pen - cil or rule.

50

Your Smiling Face

Words and Music by
JAMES TAYLOR

*To play along with recording, place capo at 4th fret.

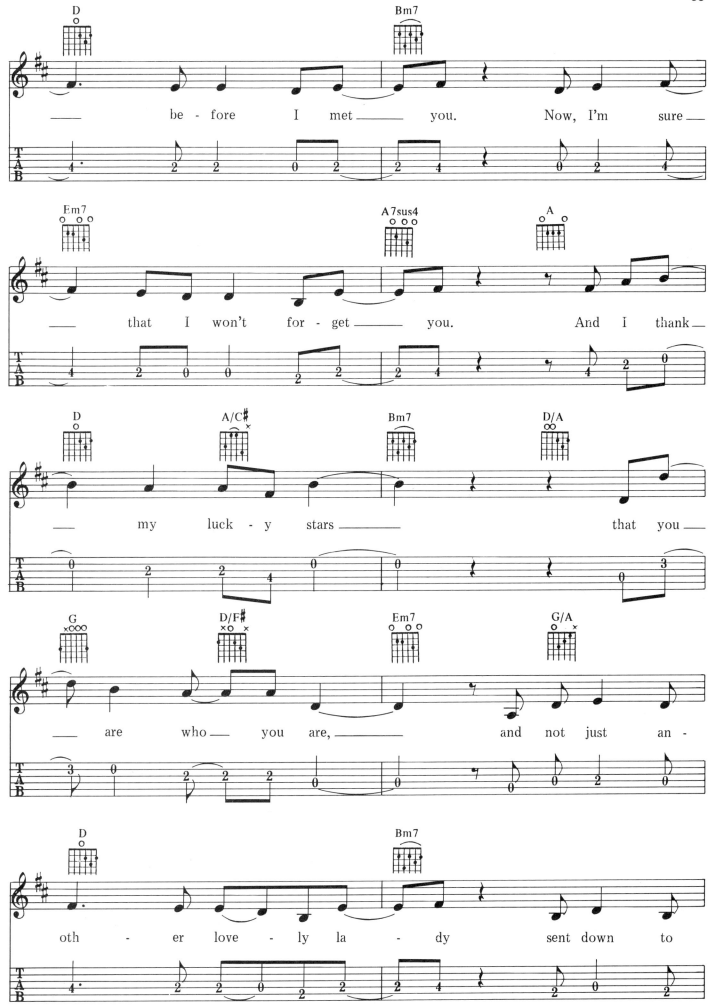

ONLY A DREAM IN RIO

Words and Music by
JAMES TAYLOR

*To play along with recording, place capo at 2nd fret.

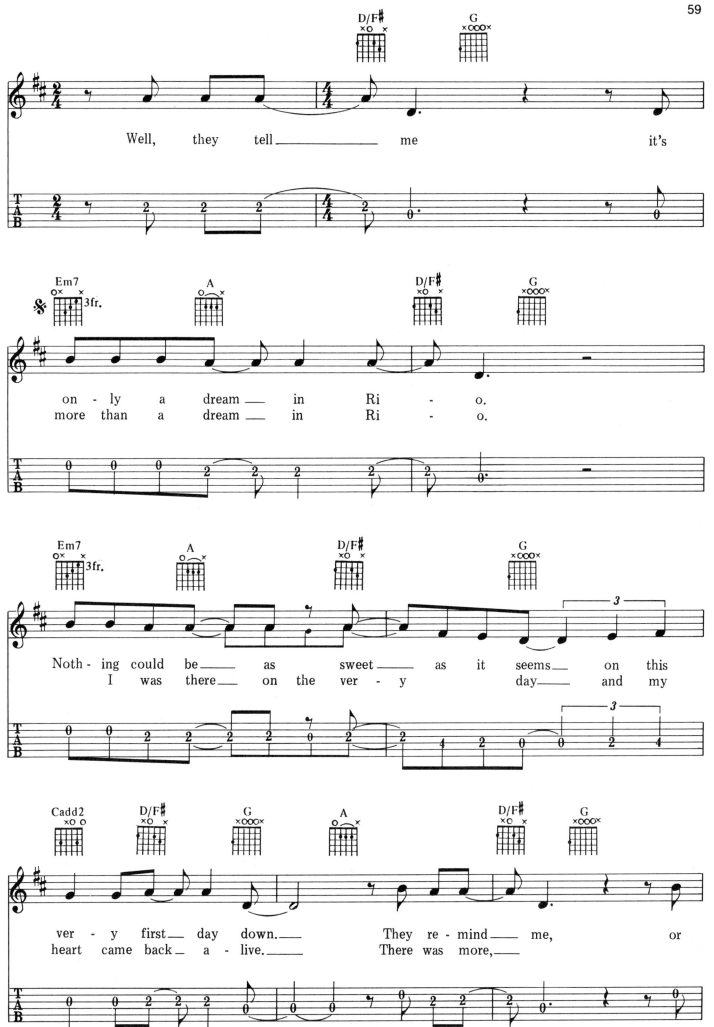

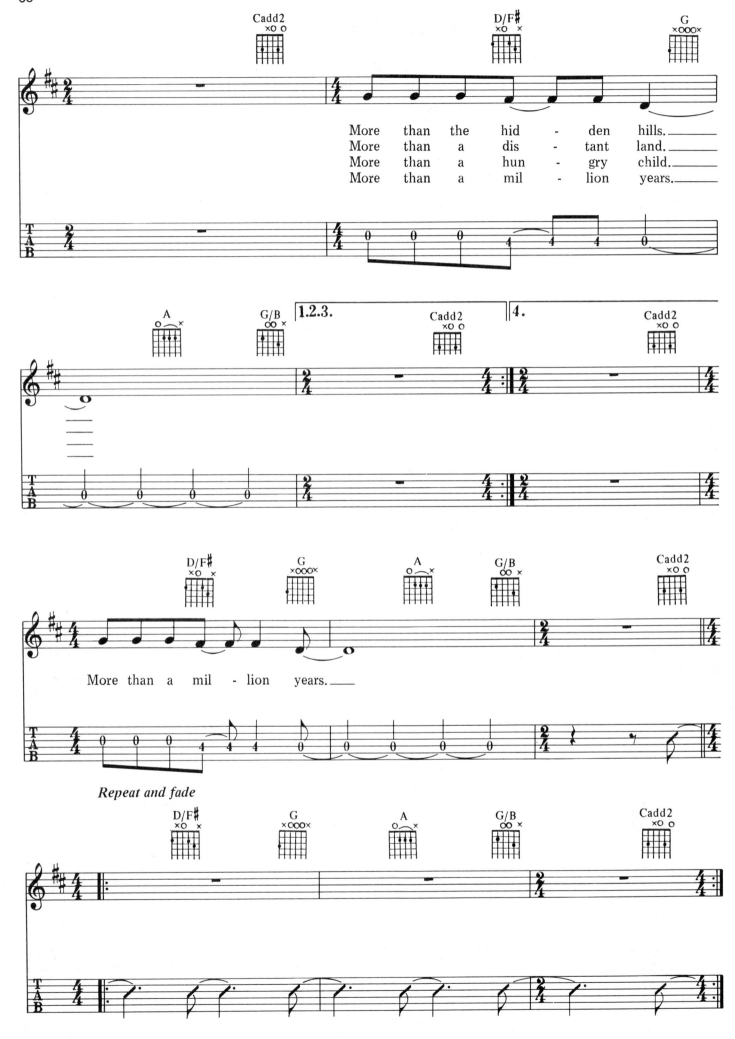

More than the hid - den hills.
More than a dis - tant land.
More than a hun - gry child.
More than a mil - lion years.

1.2.3.

4.

More than a mil - lion years.

Repeat and fade

Bartender's Blues

Words and Music by
JAMES TAYLOR

* To play along with recording, place capo at first fret.

70

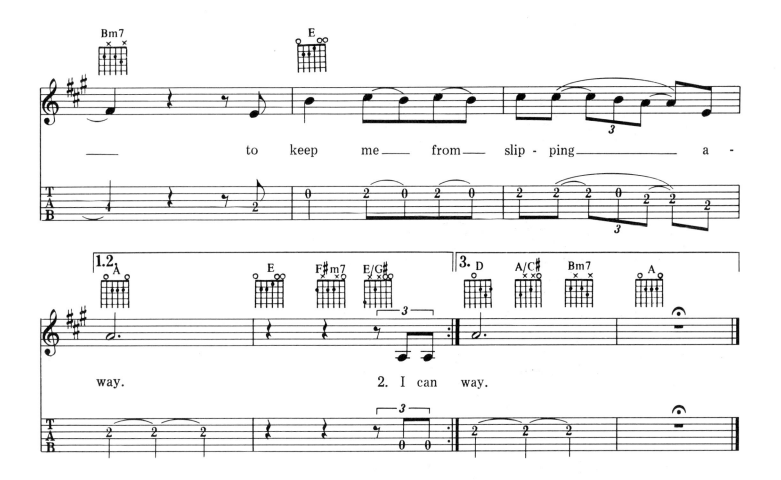

to keep me from slip - ping a -

way.   2. I can way.

Additional Lyrics.

2. I can light up your smokes, I can laugh at your jokes.
   I can watch you fall down on your knees.
   I can close down this bar, I can gas up my car.
   I can pack up and mail in my key. *(To Chorus)*

3. Now the smoke fills the air in this honky-tonk bar.
   And I'm thinking 'bout where I'd rather be.
   But I burned all my bridges, I sank all my ships,
   And I'm stranded at the edge of the sea. *(To Chorus)*

HOW SWEET IT IS
(To Be Loved By You)

Words and Music by
EDDIE HOLLAND, LAMONT DOZIER
and BRIAN HOLLAND

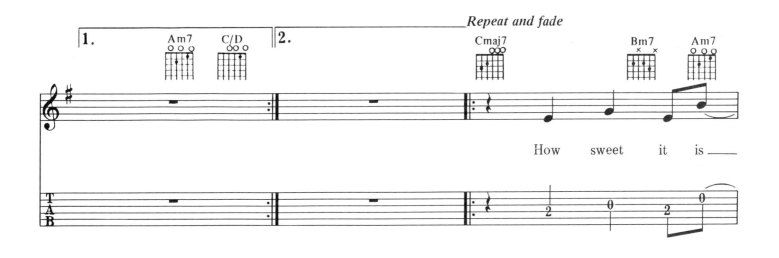

How sweet it is ___

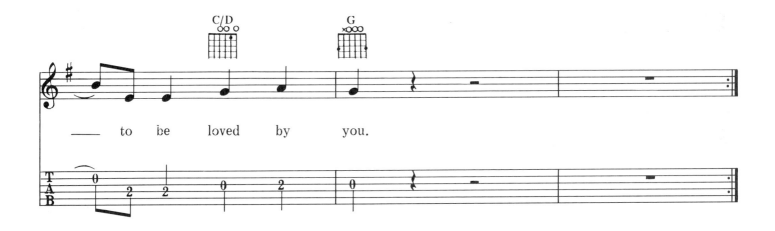

___ to be loved by you.

Additional Lyrics

2. I close my eyes at night,
Wondering where would I be without you in my life.
Everything I did was just a bore,
Everywhere I went, seems I'd been there before.
But you brighten up for me all of my days
With a love so sweet in so many ways.
I want to stop, *etc.*

3. *Instrumental (8 bars)*
You were better to me than I was to myself.
For me there's you and there ain't nobody else.
I want to stop, *etc.*

Limousine Driver

Words and Music by
JAMES TAYLOR

*To play along with recording, place capo at 3rd fret.

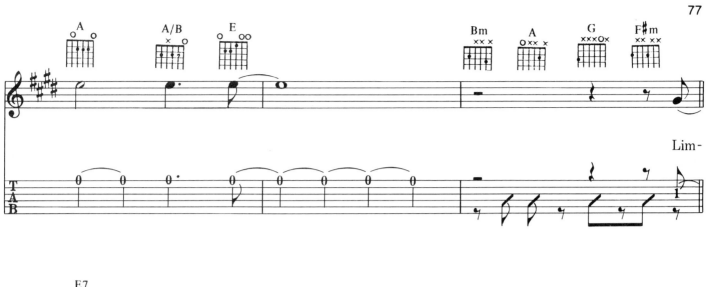

Lim-

ou - sine driv - er. Big
ing through the jun - gle. Get your

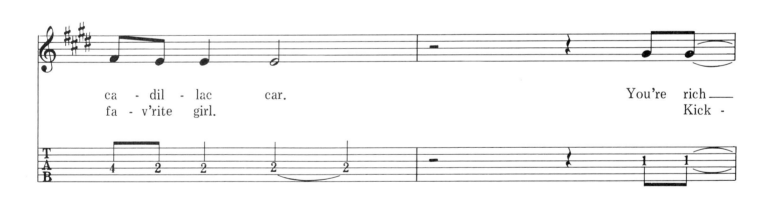

ca - dil - lac car. You're rich___
fa - v'rite girl. Kick -

___ and you're fa - mous.___ Know what a
in' off a bun - dle.___ Go on and

fool   you   are,   you   are.   Seen   a
give   it   a   shove.   Pick   up,

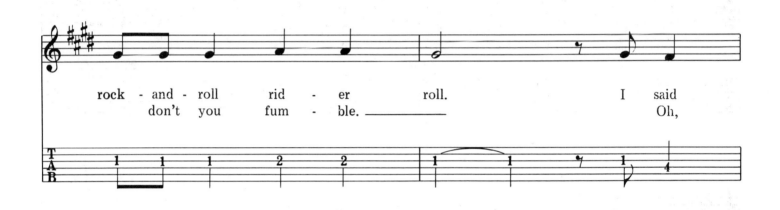

rock - and - roll   rid - er   roll.   I   said
don't   you   fum - ble.   Oh,

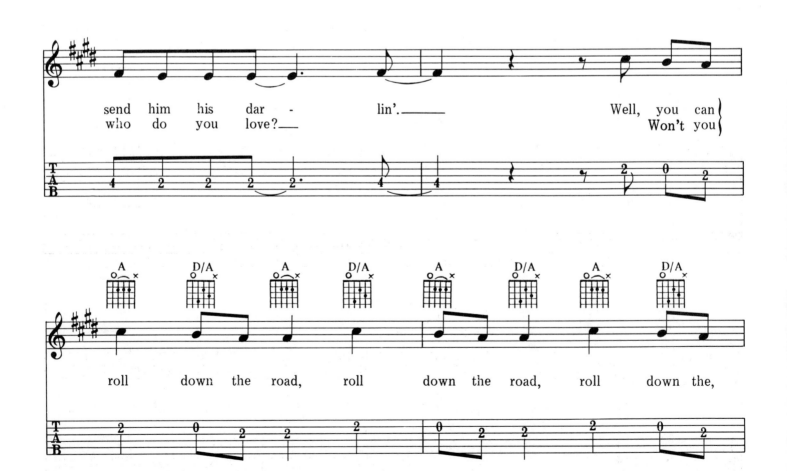

send   him   his   dar -   lin'.   Well, you can
who   do   you   love?   Won't you

roll   down   the   road,   roll   down   the   road,   roll   down   the,

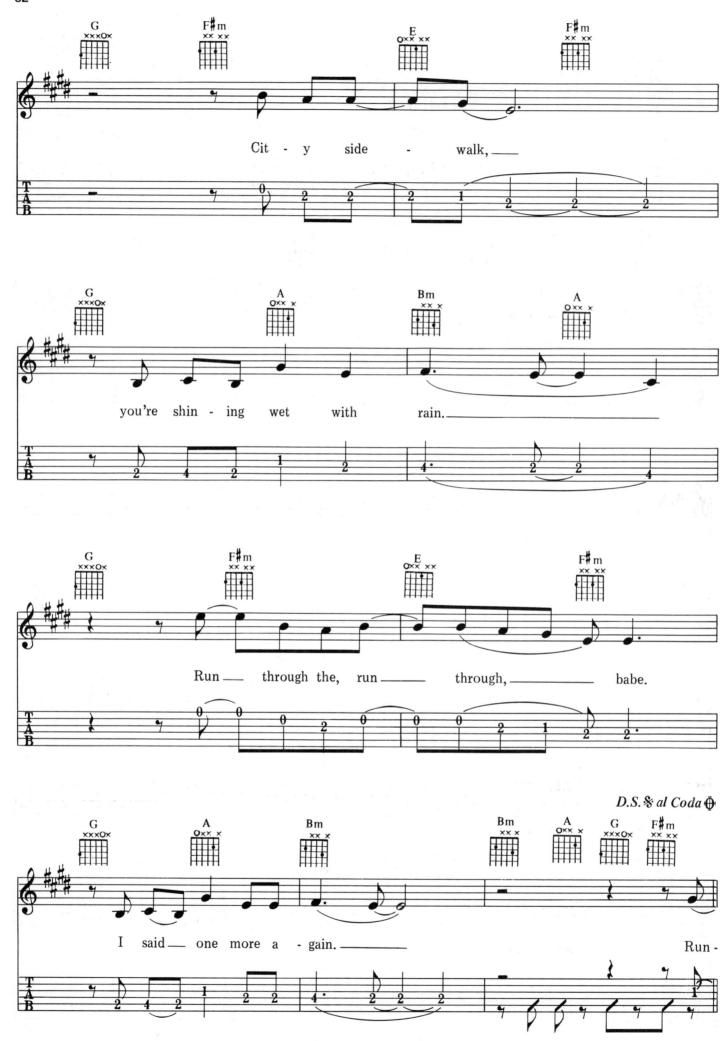

Mona

Words and Music by
JAMES TAYLOR

*To play along with recording, place capo at 2nd fret.

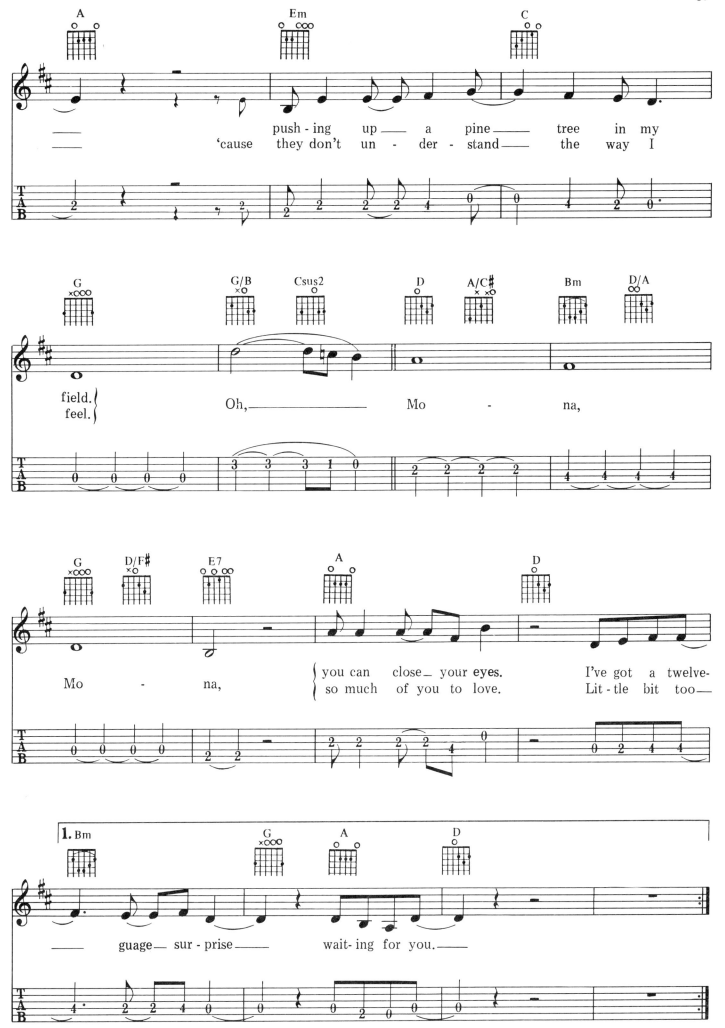